CW00822698

THE YORKSHIRE COAST FROM THE AIR

by

Trevor Sanderson

HUTTON PRESS
2003

Published by

The Hutton Press Ltd.,
130 Canada Drive, Cherry Burton,
Beverley, East Yorkshire
HU17 7SB

Copyright © Photographs and Text
Trevor Sanderson 2003

No part of this book may be reproduced, stored in a retrieval system or transmitted
in any form, or by any means electronic, mechanical, photocopying, recording or
otherwise without the prior consent of the Publisher and the Copyright holder.

Printed by

Intellectual Print.
Unit 2, Swann Street Unit Factory Estate,
Swann Street, Hull HU2 0PH
Tel: 01482 222778
www.intellectualprint.co.uk

CONTENTS

Preface

The Yorkshire Coast has always had a special fascination for me. Born and brought up in Beverley, it was probably our family holidays in Scarborough every year which awoke my interest in it. Having explored the coast by foot, by bicycle, by car, by boat, and even underwater, I realise that it is perhaps only from the air that the enormous variety and beauty of our coast can be fully appreciated.

In the course of taking the photographs and doing the research for the captions, I have had the pleasure of visiting most, if not all, of the places featured in the photographs, and of meeting and talking to many interesting people along the way. Thank you, to all of you, too numerous to mention, at the various information centres, nature centres, libraries, museums, buildings, churches, farms, cafés, restaurants, inns, hotels, holiday homes, shops, lifeboat stations, coastguard stations, coastal and industrial establishments for the help and information so freely given, without which this book would not have been possible.

I would like to thank Charles Brook of Hutton Press for his continued encouragement in the publishing of this book, and to all those who have helped in the production of it. The co-owners of our aircraft, Alberto, Guy and Robert, for help with the flying. My colleagues in the Estec Flying Club for much help on the subject of aerial photography. Glenn Jones, his wife, and members of the Hull Aero Club for hospitality at Beverley Airport during the taking of most of the photographs. My sister Rosemary Turner and husband David for acting as safety pilots during many of the photo-taking flights. Finally, my wife Maggie and children Caroline and Michael for their help and patience, and my father and late mother for their love of Yorkshire.

About the author

Trevor Sanderson was born in Beverley in the East Riding of Yorkshire, and has had a keen interest in the Yorkshire Coast ever since his very first visit to the coast with his parents and sister during their summer holidays in Scarborough. Since then he has explored most of the coast on foot, by bicycle, car, boat, and even underwater.

He was educated at Beverley Grammar School, and then gained a B.Sc. in physics and a Ph.D. in cosmic ray physics from Imperial College in London. He is currently employed as a Senior Research Scientist at the European Space Agency's Research and Technology Centre in the Netherlands. It was in Holland that he learned to fly. Now the owner, together with an Italian, a Dutch, and a French colleague of a light aircraft, he regularly flies back to the UK and Yorkshire. Flying into Beverley's Linley Hill airfield, it is from there that he now explores, from the air, the Yorkshire Coast.

The author of the successful book, "Beverley from the Air", he now turns his attention to the sea with this book of stunning photographs of the Yorkshire Coast from Spurn Point to Staithes.

Spurn Head. The most southerly point on the Yorkshire Coast and one of three Heritage Coasts in Yorkshire. Spurn Head is made up of material such as sand and shingle which has been eroded from the cliffs of Holderness, washed down the coast, and deposited here. At low tide, much of this material is exposed, giving rise to the wide expanse of sands seen here. Spurn is connected to the mainland at Kilnsea by the narrow strip of land at the top of the picture. Just visible at the top left are the North Sea Gas Terminals at Easington.

Spurn Point. Spurn Point is home to Associated British Port's Vessels Traffic Services, the Humber Lifeboat, the Humber Pilots and two lighthouses. Both the old and the new lighthouses visible here are no longer in use. The long jetty ensures that both the pilot vessels, one of which is seen here leaving the jetty, can put to sea at any state of the tide. Moored offshore is the R.N.L.I. all-weather Humber Lifeboat, *Pride of the Humber*, one of the few in Britain manned by a full time crew.

Spurn Point. The large white building in the centre is Associated British Port's Vessels Traffic Services Centre. Here, two Assistant Habour masters control the traffic all the way along the river, and coordinate the activities of the Humber Pilots. Behind, to the left, are the Coastguard offices, and to the right, the accommodation and offices of the lifeboat crews.

Spurn Nature Reserve. Spurn is an important staging point for migrating birds. In 1960 the Yorkshire Wildlife Trust became the owner of the peninsula and established a bird ringing station and a laboratory here at The Warren. Spurn is now a National Nature Reserve, and is managed with the help of English Nature and the Spurn Heritage Coast Project. This view of the northern entrance to Spurn shows the Trust's buildings, which include an information centre, accommodation, and a bird ringing station.

North Sea Gas Terminals. BP's Easington terminal, at bottom right, was built in 1967, and was Britain's first terminal to receive gas. In the centre is British Gas's Rough Facility, now owned by Dynegy, which manages a gas storage facility in the depleted Rough Field in the North Sea. At the top is BP's Dimlington terminal.

Withernsea. An old Holderness village which developed into a holiday resort after the opening of the railway line from Hull. The railway is long gone, and the old station is now a nursery, just visible below the car park left of centre, next to St. Nicholas church and the Pavilion Leisure Centre. The white roofed building in the centre is a supermarket, built on the site of the old railway sidings. In the centre of the picture, alongside the Valley Gardens, are two stacks on the edge of the beach, all that remains of Withernsea's Pier. The pier was dismantled in 1903 after a number of vessels had collided with it.

Withernsea Lighthouse. In the middle of a housing estate, is Withernsea's lighthouse, now a museum. It has Coastguard and R.N.L.I. exhibits, a local history room, and a memorial to Withernsea's famous actress, Kay Kendall. From the top, on a clear day, there is a magnificent view of the coastline of Holderness.

Hornsea. Another old Holderness village which owes its growth to the coming of the railway line. In the middle of the picture is the new Leisure Centre, alongside which is a boat yard for small fishing boats. To the left is Wilbur's Market. The Police station, situated next to Station Court, is on the site of the old railway station.

Hornsea Mere. The last remaining of the many ancient meres of Holderness. Now part of the mere is a nature reserve owned by the R.S.P.B., and a site of special scientific interest. Swan Island is on the left of the picture, and Kirkholme Point, home of Hornsea Sailing Club is on the right. St Mary's Church, Hall Garth Park and the town centre are between the Mere and the sea.

Hornsea and the Mere. The main shopping street, Newbegin, runs from bottom centre of the picture into the Market Place on the right. Alongside, on a small mound, is the beautiful St. Mary's Church, built with cobbles and stones taken from the beach and completed in the 16th century. Just below the church is part of Hall Garth Park and the Hall. The award-winning Hornsea Folk Museum is to the left of the Hall. Kirkholme Point, on The Mere, home of Hornsea Sailing Club, is at the top of the picture.

Hornsea Freeport. Seen here on a busy Sunday in August, Hornsea Freeport began life as Hornsea Pottery, and is now a thriving discount shopping centre. Attractions here include a shopping mall, shops, Butterfly World, the Bird of Prey Centre, and a model village. Alongside is the track of the old Hull to Hornsea railway line, now a footpath and part of the Trans Pennine Trail.

Skipsea and Skirlington. One of the Yorkshire coast's many holiday home developments makes an interesting pattern when seen from the air. In the foreground, another nine more holes are being added to Skipsea's golf course, alongside the Far Grange Holiday Camp. Beyond is Skirlington Holiday Homes, on Sundays, home to Skirlington Market. Beyond that are several of Scottish and Southern's underground storage caverns, in which gas from the North Sea is stored. From here the coastline continues south past Hornsea and the Mere and sweeps round towards Spurn Point. To the right is the Far Grange's McCann Wildlife Trust country park, winner of a David Bellamy Gold Award.

Fraisthorpe Beach. Not far from Bridlington is Fraisthorpe Beach. With parking right on the cliff top, it is a favourite place for a family day out. A small stream, Auburn Beck, winds its way around past Auburn Farm on the left of the picture, before discharging into the sea. This is the site of the medieval village of Auburn which disappeared into the sea many years ago. On the right of the picture is the Elim Pentecostal Church's annual youth and children's camp, held here every year.

Bridlington. It's a glorious Sunday afternoon at the end of August. The tide is on its way out, the sands are slowly drying out, and the water is warm. The sea is blue, and the white cliffs of Flamborough and Bridlington's golden sands are brilliantly illuminated by the afternoon sun. It's a beautiful day to be by the sea.

Bridlington South Sands. As the tide recedes, it leaves behind a wide stretch of firm dry sands. At this state of the tide, only half of the beach is exposed. The Spa, on the promenade, is right of centre. Near the top of the picture, the Priory Church stands out proudly above the buildings of the Old Town, beyond which are the rolling hills of the Wolds.

Bridlington Spa. For years, one of the East Riding's premier entertainment centres. The Spa Royal Hall is in the centre of the picture, to the left of which is the Spa Theatre. Behind the Spa Theatre is Bridlington's Lifeboat Station. Bridlington is home to the *Marine Engineer*, an all-weather lifeboat, and the *Lord Feoffees III*, an inshore rescue boat.

Bridlington Harbour. At low tide the harbour dries out, and Gypsey Race, a small stream which rises in the Wolds, flows sporadically into the harbour. On both sides of the harbour, a large expanse of firm sand is exposed. The harbour is enclosed by the North and the South Piers, with Chicken Run Jetty in the middle. The South Pier is home to Bridlington's commercial fishing activities. The harbour is also home to the Royal Yorkshire Yacht Club and many pleasure boats. Behind the harbour is the area known as Bridlington Quay, the shopping and commercial centre of Bridlington.

The Esplanade. Running parallel to the sea wall is the Esplanade. On the sea front, next to the fun fair, is the Forum Cinema, on the site of the old Floral Pavilion. The elegant white terraced houses of Cliff Street, The Crescent, and Marlborough Terrace connect the Esplanade with the Promenade behind. The domed glass roof building is the new Promenade Shopping Centre.

Bridlington North Sands. Being closer to the town centre, the North Sands are probably the more popular of the two beaches. Just left of centre is Leisure World, built on the site of the Grand Pavilion. The elegant buildings of the Royal Crescent and Albion Terrace are on the right of the picture, a vivid contrast to the rows of small terraced houses behind. Behind Albion Terrace is the Holy Trinity Church.

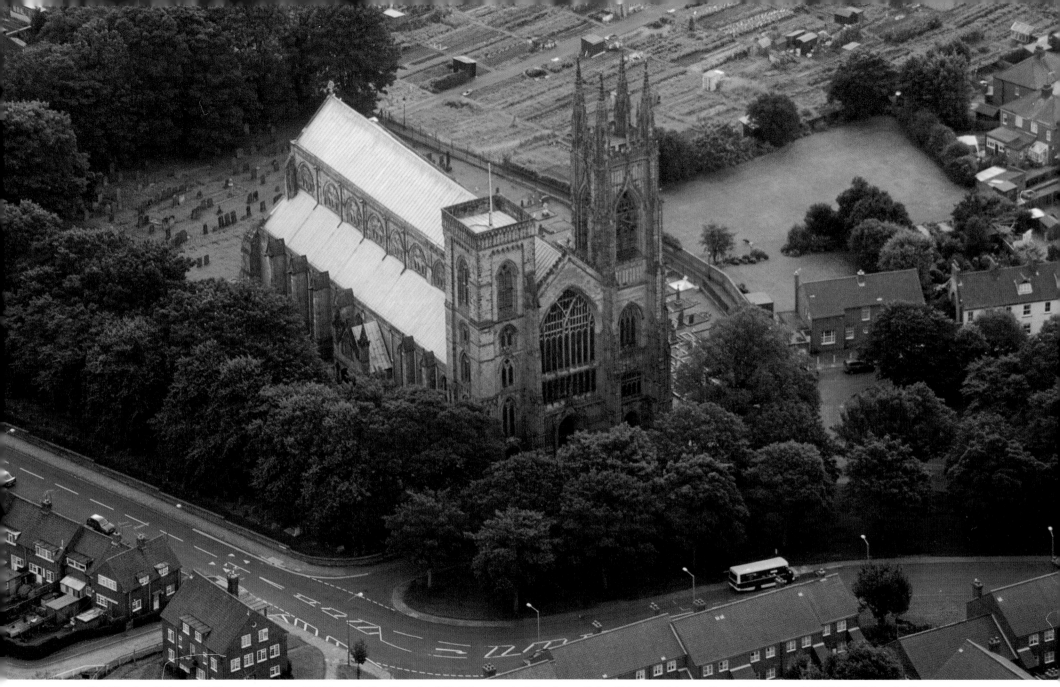

Bridlington Priory. Hidden away in the Old Town is the Church of St. Mary, part of the Augustinian Priory which was founded in around 1100 by Walter de Gaunt, the son of one of William the Conqueror's men. Most of the Priory has now disappeared, the monastery having been dissolved by Henry VIII in 1537, leaving only the nave of the church and the Bayle Gate. Re-built in the 19th century, the church has one on the finest west windows and largest organs in the north of England.

Bayle Gate. Probably the original gate house of Bridlington Priory, Bayle Gate, owned by the Lords Feoffees and Assistants of the Manor of Bridlington, is now a museum containing displays and articles from the Middle ages up to the present time. It is hidden away in a charming tree-lined square in front of the Priory, not far from the centre of the Old Town. The road at the top right of the picture, High Street, leads off into the Market Place and the centre of the Old Town.

Sewerby. Once a stately home, Sewerby Hall and Park is now owned by East Riding of Yorkshire Council. The Hall is surrounded by magnificent gardens, which include many rare and exotic trees. Behind the Hall is the Large Formal garden, and to the right is the English garden. On this Sunday afternoon, cricket and bowls are being played on the cliff top. At the bottom of the cliff are the remains of a pre-historic beach, within which elephant and rhinoceros bones have been found.

Sewerby Hall. The Hall contains a museum of East Yorkshire, an art gallery, and trophies and items relating to Amy Johnson, the first woman to fly solo to Australia. Behind are the formal gardens, within which are many exotic trees, including several 200-year-old monkey-puzzle trees, reputed to be some of the oldest in the country.

Sewerby, the English Garden. The patterns of the rose and bedding plants in this walled garden are surely best seen from the air. To the right is the herb garden. Behind and to the left are the large formal gardens.

Flamborough Head. Another of Yorkshire's Heritage Coasts, this view shows the whole of the Flamborough Head Heritage Coast, ranging from Bempton Cliffs at the top left all the way round to Sewerby at the bottom left. The wooded Danes Dyke runs all the way across the middle of the headland, seemingly cutting off Flamborough village, on the right of the picture, from the mainland. At Sewerby the boulder clay cliffs of Holderness give way to chalk cliffs of Flamborough Head, brilliantly illuminated by the afternoon Sun.

Danes Dyke. Seemingly cutting Flamborough Head in two, Danes Dyke extends all the way across Flamborough Head. Named after the Danes, it was most likely not constructed by them, but by Iron Age man. The southern part is a natural ravine, or wyke, within which a small stream, fed by numerous springs, runs down to the sea. The northern part consists of substantial man-made fortifications. Bridlington Links Golf Course is to the left of the ravine and Flamborough village on the right.

South Landing. Close-up of South Landing, another wooded ravine. A small spring-fed stream flows down the ravine. South Landing is home to the Flamborough inshore rescue lifeboat. The lifeboat station is at the bottom of the ravine on the left. Beacon Hill, one of the highest points of Flamborough Head, is on the left of the ravine.

Flamborough Head. The white chalk cliffs on this part of the headland are covered with a thick layer of boulder clay, which gives rise to the rounded appearance of the cliff tops. The tide is a long way out and most of the rocks at the foot of the cliffs are exposed. The waters here are much clearer and bluer than in other parts of the country, due to the lack here of any major rivers discharging their suspended matter into the sea. In the spring many of the fields in this part of Yorkshire are sown with rape seed, giving rise to a patchwork of different coloured fields.

Flamborough Lighthouse. This close-up of Flamborough Head and the lighthouses from the south shows the modern lighthouse, which dates from 1806. The lighthouse is now unmanned and monitored remotely from the Trinity House Operations Control Centre in Harwich. Behind and to the left is the old Beacon Tower, dating from the 17th century, made out of local chalk. Behind and to the right is the Flamborough Golf Course, the undulating surface accentuated by the late afternoon sunshine. In the foreground, almost cut off from the headland, is the rock formation known as High Stacks.

Selwicks Bay. Early in the morning, it's high tide, and the sea is calm and still. A lone coble is already out fishing in the bay. Selwicks Bay, at the tip of Flamborough Head is to the right of the picture.

Flamborough Lighthouse. Close up of the lighthouses, the Fog Station and Selwicks Bay.

North Landing. The tide is out, and the car park is just filling up in this early morning picture. On the left, in the headland next to North Landing, is Robin Lythe's cave, reachable via the rocks at low tide, or by boat at high tide. Carved into the chalk by the action of waves and water are a multitude of interesting inlets and caves, no doubt in the past, a smuggler's paradise.

Thornwick Bay. Early in the morning, and the bay is deserted. From the café on top of the cliff, a small path leads down to the rocky headland. The tide is out, and the rocks and small caves in the headland between Thornwick Bay and Little Thornwick Bay are exposed and waiting to be explored. Behind are the caravans and holiday homes of Thornwick and Sea Farm Holiday Centre.

Danes Dyke. The man-made part of Danes Dyke consists of huge embankments, flanked by trees. It crosses this part of the headland in an almost straight line, reaching the coast at Cat Nab. The almost vertical cliffs here are 300 feet high, and no longer have a thick layer of boulder clay on top. Behind and to the right are the villages of Bempton and Buckton

Bempton Cliffs. Home to a multitude of seabirds, including Auks, Fulmars, Razorbills and Shearwaters, it is the only place on the east coast of England where the rarer Puffin and Gannet nest. Once 'Climmers' from the nearby villages would collect the seabirds' eggs, climbing down the cliffs on ropes. It is now a nature reserve owned by the Royal Society for the Protection of Birds. The visitor centre and car park is on the left of the picture. On the right are the remains of the cliff-top RAF Bempton radar station, once an important part of the country's early warning system.

Buckton Cliffs. The northern edge of the chalk cliffs of Flamborough continue on inland here, as Buckton's sheer 400 foot high chalk cliffs give way to the sloping boulder clay cliffs of Filey Bay. The edge of the chalk deposit disappears inland as a ridge which becomes Speeton Hills, and continues on towards Staxton and Ganton, on the edge of the Vale of Pickering. Sitting on top of the ridge is Speeton Village, right of centre.

Speeton Gap. Here the chalk cliffs give way to the boulder clay cliffs at the point where Filey bay begins. Speeton Beck, a small stream fed by a spring, flows down Speeton Gap, a beautiful wooded ravine, which cuts through the Speeton Cliffs and runs down to Speeton Sands on the right of the picture. Speeton village is perched on top of a boulder clay ridge on the edge of the chalk cliffs. The old Coastguard Station, now a private residence, on top of one of the highest points, is in the middle of the picture.

Reighton Gap. On the top of the boulder clay cliffs south of Filey is Haven's Reighton Sands Holiday Village. A small ravine, Reighton Gap, descends down to the beach. Alongside on the right is an old track which runs down to the beach. On this stretch of coast the 15-foot skeleton of a 130 million-year-old Plesiosaur was found recently, soon to be displayed in one of Scarborough's museums. Further inland, on the main road from Bridlington to Filey, is the village of Reighton.

Primrose Valley. Not far from Filey and close to the site of the former Butlin's Holiday Camp is Primrose Valley Holiday Village, another popular holiday resort. In front is the hamlet of Flat Cliffs, seemingly clinging to the edge of the cliffs.

Filey. A fine view of Filey and its bay taken from a vantage point high over the bay. Carr Naze and Filey Brigg extend out into the North Sea on the right. It's high tide, and the Brigg is only just visible. Further up the coast are Newbiggin Cliffs, Grisethorpe Bay, Cayton Bay, and Scarborough, the coastline continuing on towards Whitby and the moors. Top left is the vale of Pickering. The white buildings of the Crescent shine brightly in the early afternoon sun, and are a landmark which can be seen from many miles away. A few summer cumulus clouds cast their shadows on the sea and on the countryside along the coast.

Filey Bay. Looking out to sea, this view shows Filey and the bay, with beyond Carr Naze and the Brigg. The tide has just turned and is on its way out and part of the Brigg is now exposed. A lone yacht is moored in the middle of the bay. Next to Carr Naze is the Country Park. The railway line, once on the edge of town, now cuts through the old and new parts of the town. In the middle is the sports ground of Filey's Sport Association.

Filey Bay. Filey is famous for its vast expanse of firm sands, seen here exposed at a low spring tide. In the distance, the headland Carr Naze shelters the bay from the worst of the North Sea's storms. Jutting out from the headland is Filey Brigg, also exposed at this state of the tide. The mysterious spittle rocks, thought by some to be the remains of a Roman harbour, show up as a dark trace half way along the Brigg.

Filey. Seen from a point high above the Brigg, the whole of the town is visible in this late spring view. It's a spring tide, and the tide is out, revealing the vast expanse of Filey's beach. In the foreground is the Country Park. Next to the Church Ravine is St Oswald's Church. At the top of the ravine is a freshwater spring, to which perhaps Filey owes its existence. At the bottom of the ravine is the Coble landing. At the far side of Filey, beyond the elegant buildings of The Crescent, is Martin Ravine.

New Filey. High up on top of the cliffs of Filey and brightly illuminated by the morning sun are the magnificent buildings of The Crescent. Developed in the 1850's together with the coming of the railway, they have a commanding view of the bay. It's high water and the beach is covered. At the water's edge is the road known as The Beach, at the end of which is a children's paddling pool. On the sloping part of the cliffs are the Crescent Gardens. On the left, just visible, are Glen Gardens. Right at the top of the picture is the Dams Nature Reserve.

Glen Gardens. At the western end of The Crescent are the Glen Gardens, built on the site of the grounds of the former Ravine Hall. The hall was demolished in the 1970's, and now a café stands on the site, alongside the boating lake. The wooded Martin Ravine leads down to the sea, separating the gardens from a miniature golf course.

The Crescent. Close-up of the southern end of the elegant Crescent. The steep Crescent Hill leads down from the Crescent to The Beach, the paddling pool and the Royal Parade. The tide is now out, and the sands are drying out. Behind the Crescent are the greens of Filey Bowling Club, the courts of Filey Lawn Tennis Club, and the headquarters of Filey Sea Scouts.

Crescent Gardens. Another close-up of the Crescent, the gardens, the bandstand and the Sun Lounge. The gardens are filled today with holidaymakers listening to a Sunday afternoon performance in the bandstand, one of Filey's traditions. Stones from the Roman Signal Station on Carr Naze are displayed here in the garden above and to the right of the bandstand.

Old Filey. Running inland from Cliff Top, on the right of the picture, is Queen Street, one of the oldest streets in Filey. On the right, the Ravine descends down to the sea, meeting The Beach on the right hand side of the picture. The small building with the large blue door on The Beach is the Coastguard Station.

Coble landing. It's full of activity here on this Sunday afternoon. The tide is going out and the beach is slowly drying off. Just a handful of cobles can be seen in amongst the boats hauled up onto the landing. Left of centre, alongside Church Ravine, is the Filey Lifeboat Station, home to the *Keep Fit Association*, an all-weather lifeboat, and the *Rotary District 1120*, an inshore rescue lifeboat.

Filey Dams Nature Reserve. Just on the edge of one of Filey's housing estates is the Filey Dams Nature Reserve, a freshwater marsh full of bird life. Leased from Scarborough Borough Council, it is managed by the Yorkshire Wildlife Trust. There are hides next to the car park, hidden in the trees at the top left of the picture, and at the edge of the largest of the pools. As well as being an important site for birds, it is home to a number of different types of mammals, insects and amphibians.

Carr Naze and The Brigg. The headland known as Carr Naze was once the site of a Roman Signal Station, most of which is now lost due to erosion and landslides. Excavated in the late 19th century, some of the remains are now in the town museum and some in the Crescent Gardens. On this side of the headland, the sea has carved out three semi-circular pools known as doodles, the most prominent of which is called The Emperor's Pool.

Grisethorpe Bay. Halfway between Filey and Scarborough is this secluded bay. In this early morning picture, the waves breaking on the half-submerged rocks, and the patterns made in the emerald-coloured sea by the different type of vegetation on the rocks and the sea bed make this a beautiful sight. Grisethorpe is famous for a Bronze-Age oak coffin and man found in 1834, now displayed in the Rotunda Museum in Scarborough.

Cayton Bay. Separated from Grisethorpe Bay by the headland known as Low Red Cliff, Cayton Bay is another of Yorkshire's beautiful bays, with a fine expanse of beach which is exposed at low tide. The headland is famous for the fossil plant beds at Yons Nab at the foot of the cliffs. On the top of the cliff above Cayton Bay, on the other side of the main Filey to Scarborough main road, is Cayton Bay Holiday Camp.

Scarborough South Cliff. This view of the cliffs of the south bay is dominated by the cliff in the foreground, which slid into the sea in 1993 as a result of a landslide, taking with it Holbeck Hall Hotel and part of Holbeck Gardens. It is now grassed over, and protected by a new sea wall. Above the South Bay Bathing Pool, now filled in, are the South Cliff Gardens, which include the wooded Italian Gardens, and the Belvedere Rose Gardens. On the top are the elegant Georgian hotels of the Esplanade.

Holbeck Gardens. Paths criss-cross the cliff in this view of the Clock Tower and putting green in Holbeck Gardens. The Clock Tower was given to the town by Alfred Shuttleworth in 1909. Behind is Redcourt, once the private residence of Alfred Shuttleworth, and now famous as the hospital in the television series "The Royal". The quiet, secluded Shuttleworth Garden, full of scented flowers, and with Braille markers for blind visitors, is on the left of the picture. At the top of the picture are the playing fields of Bramcote School.

The Spa Complex. The Spa has always played an important part in Scarborough's social and entertainment life. Healing waters were discovered here in the 1600's and various buildings have existed on this site. The existing buildings, dating from around one hundred years ago, have recently been refurbished, and are now know as the Spa Complex. The Complex includes the Spa Theatre, the Ocean Ballroom, and the Clock Café. Above, on the top of the cliffs, are the elegant hotels of the Esplanade. On the left is the South Cliff Tramway, the oldest in the country.

Valley Gardens. One of the main ways into the South Bay is Valley Road, on either side of which are the Valley gardens. The valley is crossed on the left of the picture by Valley Bridge. In the foreground, the Spa Bridge, a footbridge, crosses from the Spa and the South Cliff on the left to St. Nicholas Cliff, alongside the Grand Hotel on the right. The terraced houses of The Crescent overlook the gardens in the middle of the picture. Beneath the Crescent and next to the Spa Bridge is Woodend, Scarborough's natural history museum. Next door is the Art Gallery, and next to that is Londesborough Lodge. To the right, next to the Spa Bridge, is the unmistakable shape of the Rotunda, Scarborough's Archaeology Museum. Falsgrave Road and Westborough run from left to right across the top part of the picture.

Oliver's Mount and The Mere. Overlooking Scarborough is Oliver's Mount, a flat-topped hill on top of which is Scarborough's War Memorial. From here there is a magnificent view of Scarborough and the Harbour. Close by the War Memorial is Oliver's Mount Café. Oliver's Mount is home to Scarborough's motorbike races. On the right, in Seamer Valley, is The Mere, a marshy lake left over from the last ice age. It is now a water sports centre.

Scarborough Harbour. The harbour and south sands seen from above the town centre. The tide is on its way out, the sea is calm, and it's a beautiful summer's afternoon. Holidaymakers are already on the beach and the foreshore road. Left of the harbour are the cliffs of Castle Hill and the old town. The Grand Hotel towers high above St. Nicholas Cliff, overlooking the bay. To the left of the Grand Hotel are the Royal Hotel and the Town Hall. Westborough and Eastborough, half in the shade, run up from the harbour to the town centre on the left of the picture.

South Sands. Another view of the south sands and the harbour, looking back towards the town and St. Nicholas Cliff. The Grand Hotel is on the left of the picture, alongside St. Nicholas Gardens. At the top of the gardens are the Royal Hotel, and the Town Hall.

The Harbour. A lone speedboat leaves the harbour, leaving behind its white wake. Enclosed by the outer West and Old Piers, the Old Harbour is home to Scarborough's commercial activities, such as fishing, shipping and pleasure boat rides, while the Outer Harbour is home to Scarborough's pleasure craft. The lighthouse is on Vincent's Pier, joined to the Old Pier by a bridge. The West Pier, also called Fish Pier, is home to Scarborough's fish merchants. Alongside is Scarborough Lifeboat Station, one of the oldest in the country, home to the *Fanny Victoria Wilkinson and Frank Stubbs,* an all-weather lifeboat, and the *John Wesley Hillard II*, an inshore rescue lifeboat.

Castle Hill. Protected on the seaward sides by steep cliffs and on the landward side by a dry moat and a wall, Scarborough Castle occupies a seemingly impregnable position on top of Castle Hill. The castle and its keep, at the top of the picture, have been the scene of several sieges or bombardments throughout the ages. The site of the Roman signal station is clearly visible on the right of the picture. North Marine Drive, connecting the North Bay with the South, has always been a popular place for a walk or a drive. Today, the car parks along its length are full. Alongside the small fairground at the bottom left of the picture is the Toll House, now a Coastguard office.

North Bay. Construction of the North Marine Drive linking the North Bay with the South was started in 1897, taking 11 years to complete. Now, 100 years later, strengthening of the sea defences is underway, using special concrete blocks called accropodes, and granite from Norway. Some of the material can be seen here piled up on the beach and rocks whilst waiting to be used. When the tide goes out, a wide expanse of sands and rocks is exposed, stretching all the way to Scalby Mills. On the left, on top of the cliff, is Scarborough Cricket Ground, surrounded on three sides by rows of terraced houses.

Northstead Manor Gardens. On top of the hill on the right are the Northstead Manor Gardens, on the site of the ancient gardens of the Northstead Manor. In the centre of the picture, next to the Corner Complex and Corner Café, is the Atlantis heated outdoor waterpark. To the left of the waterpark is the entrance to the North Bay Miniature Railway, hidden in the trees, which runs from Northstead to Scalby Mills, past the site of the old Open Air Theatre. At the bottom left, on top of the cliff, are the outdoor bowling greens of the Alexandra Bowling Centre.

Peasholm Park. Perhaps best known for the model boat naval warfare battles held here twice weekly in the season. Concerts are held here on the floating bandstand on Sundays in the summer. The park is also a popular boating lake, but in this early morning view, there is nobody out on the lake yet. The lake is on the site of the ancient Northstead Manor. The lordship of Northstead Manor is retained by the Crown. MP's can resign by applying for stewardship of the Manor of Northstead, just as with the Chiltern Hundreds. The lake is fed with water from Peasholm Beck, which rises in nearby Raincliffe Woods, and descends down through Peasholm Glen, on the right of the picture, through a series of miniature lakes and waterfalls into the main lake. In the Glen are a model boat pond and a putting green.

Scalby Mills. Accessible by foot along North Bay Promenade, by miniature railway or by road along Scalby Mills Road, is Scarborough Sea Life and Marine Sanctuary, one of Scarborough's most popular attractions. When the tide is out, a wide expanse of rock and rock pools, waiting to be explored, is exposed. Scalby Beck runs down to the sea along a wooded ravine before turning inside the headland and discharging into the sea alongside the Old Scalby Mills Pub.

Hayburn Wyke. A delightfully secluded little bay, just a few miles north of Scarborough. Hayburn Beck flows down to the sea here though a wooded ravine, winding around from the bottom of the picture to the top, and ending in a small waterfall in the bay at the water's edge. The ravine is now a nature reserve owned by the National Trust, and protected as a Site of Special Scientific Interest. On the right of the picture is the Hayburn Wyke Hotel, supposedly the haunt of smugglers in times gone by. The old railway line from Scarborough to Whitby, now a wooded cycle and walking path, passes in front of the hotel.

Beast Undercliff. Between Hayburn Wyke and Ravenscar are the ledges, halfway down the cliffs, known as undercliffs. The undercliffs are inaccessible, but full of small spring-fed streams and lakes, lush vegetation and abundant wildlife. The wooded area in the foreground is the Beast Undercliff, alongside which is the Common Undercliff, just before Blea Wyke Point. Beyond, just before Robin Hood's Bay, is the headland known as Old Peak, on top of which is the village of Ravenscar.

Ravenscar. This view from the sea shows the enormous 650-foot high cliffs at Ravenscar. Blea Wyke Point is in the middle foreground, on the right of which is the undercliff known as Theil Coomb. In the middle of the picture, on top of Old Peak, one of the highest cliffs on the Yorkshire coast is Raven Hall Hotel. Behind Old Peak is Robin Hood's Bay. On the left of the picture, is the village of Ravenscar, behind which, on Stoupe Brow, are the disused quarries of the Peak Alum Works.

Raven Hall Hotel and the Peak Alum quarries. Built on the site of a fifth century Roman signal station, the first Raven Hall was opened in 1774. The current building seen here dates from 1895. Behind are the quarries of the Peak Alum Works, established here in around 1650, which were producing alum until around 1860. The quarries and the site of the alum works are now owned by the National Trust. Alum was an important ingredient in tanning and dyeing. Alum shale quarried here was turned into alum crystals in huge works located near here. The track of the old Scarborough to Whitby railway line, now a popular footpath, cuts across the bottom of the quarries.

Ravenscar and Robin Hood's Bay. The view of Robin Hood's Bay from Ravenscar is one of the most beautiful in all of Yorkshire. Raven Hall is on the right of the picture, on top of the headland, and the village of Ravenscar on the left. The town of Robin Hood's Bay is near the top centre of the picture, beyond which is Whitby. Alongside Raven Hall is the National Trust Coastal Centre, near where the track of the old railway line emerges from a tunnel. The line sweeps around, passing under the alum quarries on the left of the picture, on the edge of Stoupe Brow. A wooded ravine runs down to the sea in the middle of the picture, beyond which is the site of the Peak Alum Works, now owned by the National Trust. From there the alum was taken down an inclined railway to a dock at the bottom of the cliffs, and transported away.

Robin Hood's Bay. At low tide, the sea bed of Robin Hood's Bay is exposed, revealing this intricate pattern of ridges, or scars, thought to be due to an up-swelling of a rock dome millions of years ago. The action of the sea has carved these semi-circular ridges in the different layers of hard and soft rock. Robin Hood's Bay seemingly follows the circular shape of this dome, sweeping round from Old Peak and the reef known as Blea Steel on the left, to the town of Robin Hood's Bay on the right. Stoupe Beck flows down the valley and wooded ravine in the middle of the picture. Half way between Stoupe Beck and Robin Hood's Bay is the wooden ravine of Boggle Hole.

Boggle Hole. Not far from Robin Hood's Bay is Mill Beck, which winds its way down to the sea through a wooded ravine. Near where the beck reaches the sea is a fine old building which was once a water mill, now the Y.H.A.'s Boggle Hole Youth Hostel.

Robin Hood's Bay. Clinging onto the steep slopes of a ravine is the town of Robin Hood's Bay. Known locally as 'Bay Town', the town has a long history of seafaring, fishing and smuggling. Over the years, many houses and cottages have fallen into the sea, but now a sea-wall, built in 1975, protects the town from the ravages of the sea. As the tide goes out, the pattern of ridges in the rocks on the seabed, known as scars, is revealed. A popular tourist destination, Robin Hood's Bay is home to an inshore lifeboat. The North York Moors Visitor Centre is located here, housed in the old Coastguard Station.

Whitby High Light and Fog Station. A couple of miles south east of Whitby is the lighthouse known as Whitby High Light, sited here to protect shipping from the nearby Whitby Rock. Built in 1858 as a pair of towers, it was modified to its present form in 1890. Now unmanned, it is controlled remotely from the Trinity House Operations Control Centre in Harwich in Essex. To the right, on top of Whitestone Point, is the fog signal station, known as Hawsker's Bull.

Whitby from the south-east. An exceptionally low tide reveals an intricate pattern in the rocks and reefs on the south-eastern approaches to Whitby. High on top of the cliff in the foreground is Whitby Lighthouse. In the centre of the picture is Saltwick Bay, bounded on the nearside by Black Nab and on the far side by Saltwick Nab. A valley in the sea floor cuts across the platform of rocks and reefs in the bay. In the distance are the twin piers at the entrance to Whitby harbour. Beyond the beaches of Whitby and Sandsend are the headlands of Sandsend Ness and Kettleness.

Saltwick Bay and Nab. A secluded bay just a short distance south east of Whitby, this seemingly insignificant bay was once the scene of much industrial activity. A large part of the headland of Saltwick Nab was excavated and removed to provide alum shale for the alum industry. Many interesting fossils were found within this shale, some of which are now in Whitby's Pannet Park Museum. Offshore is a reef which is only exposed at the very lowest state of the tide, within which is a thin seam of jet. The seam, now worked out, was the source for much of the jet which was once one of the major industries of the Whitby area. On top of the cliff is Whitby Holiday Park.

Whitby. Built on a fault line through which the river Esk flows, the difference between the two sides of Whitby is clearly visible here. The older part of the town is built on the edge of the steeper East Cliff, on the left of the picture, on top of which is Whitby Abbey and St Mary's Church. The newer part of the town is on the West Cliff. When the tide is out, an extensive platform of rocks under the East Cliff, and a wide expanse of sands under the West Cliff are revealed. The Esk flows from the top right of the picture to the middle left, winding its way through the beautiful Esk valley, passing Sleights and Ruswarp and then Whitby, before finally discharging into the sea between Whitby's twin piers. At the top of the picture, on the edge of the North York Moors National Park, is Blue Bank. The Pickering to Whitby road descends here into Sleights down one of the steepest hills in Yorkshire.

Whitby. Looking out to sea from high above Ruswarp in the Esk valley. The river Esk winds around on its way to Whitby and the sea, passing under the railway viaduct which was once the main Whitby to Scarborough line, now a cycle path. It continues on past the yachts and pleasure boats moored in the Marina, once the site of Whitby's shipbuilding wharves, before reaching the harbour, the piers, and the sea. Whitby Abbey is on the top of the East Cliff to the right of the harbour.

Whitby Abbey. High on top of the East Cliff is Whitby's famous Abbey. The original Abbey was founded in the 7th century by St. Hilda, and was one of the earliest seats of learning in the country. As well as Hilda, the Abbey is famous for the Synod of Whitby, which chose the Roman method of fixing the date of Easter instead of the Celtic one, and for the poet, Caedmon, who lived here. The original Abbey buildings were destroyed by the Danes in the 9th century and lay in ruins until the coming of the Normans in the 11th century, when the Abbey was rebuilt. The Abbey prospered for hundreds of years until the dissolution of the monasteries by Henry VIII in the 16th century. On the right, overlooking the harbour is St. Mary's Church, reached from the town by a path with 199 steps.

Whitby Abbey. The Abbey, with the new Visitor Centre in Abbey House in the foreground. After the dissolution of the monasteries, the Abbey and its land were bought by the Cholmley family, who rebuilt Abbey House. It was ruined in a storm in the 18th century and never rebuilt. The magnificent banqueting hall has recently been rebuilt, and now houses the new Visitor Centre. Abbey farm is at the top of the picture.

Whitby. This view from the west at low tide shows the vast expanse of Whitby's beautiful west beach. On the right, in the foreground, is the part of Whitby known as Castle Park, next to which are the grounds of Whitby Cricket Club and Whitby Town Football Club. In the middle right of the picture, on top of the West Cliff is Whitby's Metropole Hotel. On the other side of the harbour is the East Cliff, on top of which is the Abbey. Beyond, the coastline continues on past Saltwick Bay and on towards High Hawskers.

Whitby. Most of the town is visible in this view from high over the West Cliff. The waters are calm in the beautifully sheltered harbour, protected by Whitby's two piers. The West Sands are in the foreground, with the Whitby Pavilion Complex nestling halfway down the cliff. On the top of the West Cliff is the Royal Crescent, alongside which is the Church of St. Hilda. On the opposite side of the harbour is the old town, perched on the edge of the East Cliff. On top of the cliff are St. Mary's Church and The Abbey. It's a busy Sunday, and the town is full of tourists. Cars are parked all along the roads and in the car parks.

The Royal Crescent. Close-up of the Crescent and the elegant buildings of the West Cliff. The estate on the west cliff was developed by George Hudson at the time of the coming of the railways to Whitby. The Royal Crescent was started in the 1850's, but only half completed. On the left, on the corner of North Terrace and East Terrace, and overlooking the Khyber Pass and the harbour, is the Royal Hotel. Opposite is Captain Cook's Monument.

The Khyber Pass. Named after the famous pass between Afghanistan and Pakistan, the Khyber Pass was built in 1848 to give access from Pier Road to the houses and hotels being developed on the top of West Cliff. East Terrace is at the top of the cliff, at the end of which is the Royal Hotel. Opposite is an arch made of the jawbones of a whale, and alongside is Captain Cook's Monument. Down below, in the harbour, a Whitby fishing vessel slowly manoeuvres alongside the Fish Quay. The two small round buildings on Battery Parade at the end of the quay were once used for storing gunpowder. To the left is the Scottish Bandstand.

Whitby Harbour. Close-up of the harbour seen from above the West Cliff. The *George and Mary Webb*, Whitby's all-weather lifeboat, is moored alongside the Fish Pier, just in front of the old lifeboat station, now a lifeboat museum. On the right, on the waterfront, is the Shambles, behind which is the old Town Hall and Market Square. Crowds of visitors are streaming across the bridge on this Sunday afternoon.

Whitby Bridge. Looking down from above the Abbey onto St. Mary's, the old town, and the harbour. Whitby Bridge connects the older east side of Whitby with the more recent west side. New Quay Road sweeps round to the left, towards the railway station, on the site of Whitby's old shipyards, where ships such as Cook's *Endeavour* were built. To the left of the bridge is Baxtergate, now only accessible to pedestrians, and to the right is Flowergate, the main streets of Whitby's old west side. On the right, the road runs along the waterfront known as St. Mary's Snaith towards the Fish Quay and Marine Parade.

Whitby. Looking down on the site of Whitby's boat-building wharves. The replica of the *Endeavour* is tied up close to the spot where the original boat was built, now the site of the railway station, a supermarket and the information centre. On the left is Whitby Bridge, joining together the two parts of the town. The white building, behind the two flagpoles on the right of the bridge, is the Captain Cook Museum.

Sandsend and Mulgrave Woods. Not far from Whitby is Sandsend. East Row Beck is on the left of the picture, and Sandsend Beck on the right. Close to East Row Beck is the entrance to Mulgrave Woods, open to the public on some of the days of the week. The road out of Sandsend crosses Sandsend Beck and climbs up Lythe Bank, another of the steepest hills in Yorkshire. Above the car park on the right is the old Sandsend railway station. To the right of the station is a footpath, now part of the Cleveland Way, which follows the track of the old railway line, below which are some old alum and jet workings. Years ago, the Whitby to Middlesbrough railway line crossed over the Sandsend Beck and the road alongside the railway station on a huge viaduct.

Kettleness. Another of the coast's headlands which was removed to satisfy man's insatiable appetite for alum shale. A considerable number of fossils were found in this headland, including the 15-foot plesiosaur which is on view in Whitby's Pannet Park Museum. Beyond is the headland of Sandsend Ness, which suffered a similar fate, and beyond that is Whitby. The track of the former Whitby to Middlesbrough railway line, now a footpath, sweeps across the headland and through the village of Kettleness, nestling on the top of the cliff. Behind the village is the site of the Roman signal station of Goldsborough.

Runswick Bay. From Kettleness, the coastline continues on past the village of Runswick Bay, sheltered from the North Sea by just a small headland, and on towards Port Mulgrave and Staithes. Beyond Staithes are the cliffs of Boulby, on top of which are Boulby's potash works.

Runswick Bay. The white houses cling precariously to the steep side of the cliff in this close-up of the town. In the late 1600s, the whole of the town, except for one house, was lost in a landslide. A sea wall, built in 1970, now protects most of it. Left of centre are the recently completed new sea defences and car parks. Runswick Bay is home to another of the Yorkshire coast's inshore lifeboats, kept in the lifeboat house near the centre of the picture.

Port Mulgrave. A small, almost deserted harbour, is all that remains of the port which was once used for transporting iron ore from the iron ore mines in Daleside a few miles inland from here. A tunnel through the headland ran as far as Borrowby Dale, and was used to bring the iron ore down to the port. Just a few fishing vessels are all that use the port now. Behind the Ship Inn at the top of the cliff is Beacon Hill, the site of yet another Roman signal station. A recent landslide is visible on the right of the picture.

Staithes. Another of the picturesque fishing villages of the Yorkshire coast, Staithes is built on the steep edges of the ravine through which Staithes Beck flows, and is protected from the worst of the North Sea storms by Cowbar Nab headland and two breakwaters. Once one of the East Coast's most important fishing villages, Staithes is now a popular tourist destination, and home to one of the Yorkshire coast's inshore rescue boats.

Staithes. Close-up of the village. The houses cling to the sides of the two ravines. Staithes Beck is on the right. The houses on the left face out to the sea, and are protected now by two breakwaters. Over the years, many houses in this part of Staithes were swept away, including the shop in which James Cook once was apprenticed.